W9-BVC-606

BARACKOBAMA

REVISED EDITION

BARACK OBAMA

REVISED EDITION

PRESIDENT FOR A NEW ERA

Marlene Targ Brill

Lerner Publications Company • Minneapolis

I want to thank Barack Obama for writing about his youth in the adult autobiography, *Dreams from My Father: A Story of Race and Inheritance.* Any quotes from him in this book come from this title, unless otherwise noted. Several people helped me enrich his story with their own memories of Obama. I appreciate the time Professor Kenneth Mack and Kelly Shapiro, Harvard Law School; Judson Miner; Pam Towill, the Hawaii State Library; and Pal Eldredge, Eric Kusunoki, Laurel Husain, and Chris McLachlin, Punahou School, took to share their early impressions of the president with me. In addition, I used magazine articles in *Time, Savoy, Harvard Magazine, Chicago* magazine, and the *New Yorker;* newspapers articles in the *Honolulu Advertiser, Star Bulletin, Chicago Sun-Times, Chicago Tribune, New York Times,* and *StreetWise;* and many websites about Indonesia, Hawaii, the election, and the schools Obama attended.

Copyright © 2009 by Marlene Targ Brill

The images in this book are used with the permission of: © Chip Somodevilla/Getty Images, p. 2; © Joe Raedle/Getty Images, p. 6; © Tom Bean, p. 9; © Charles E. Rotkin/CORBIS, p. 11; © Yann Arthus-Bertrand/CORBIS, p. 13; © G.E. Kidder Smith/CORBIS, p. 14; © Joseph Sohm; Visions of America/CORBIS, p. 16; AP Photo/Seth Perlman, pp. 18, 37; © Co Rentmeester/Time & Life Pictures/ Getty Images, p. 20; Punahou School Archives, p. 22; Seth Poppel Yearbook Library, pp. 23, 25; © Ralf-Finn Hestoft/CORBIS, p. 28; REUTERS/Thomas Mukoya, p. 31; © Steve Liss/Time & Life Pictures/Getty Images, p. 33; 1988 Harvard Law School Yearbook, Courtesy of Special Collections, Harvard Law School Library, p. 34; © Robyn Beck/AFP/Getty Images, p. 39; © Ted Schurter/ WireImage/Getty Images, p. 41; © William Thomas Cain/Getty Images, p. 42; © Charles Ommanney/ Getty Images, p. 43; © Mark Wilson/Getty Images, p. 44.
Front Cover: © Joe Raedle/Getty Images (main); © Stan Honda/AFP/Getty Images (background).

All rights reserved. International copyright secured. No part of this book may be reproduced, stored in a retrieval system, or transmitted in any form or by any means—electronic, mechanical, photocopying, recording, or otherwise—without the prior written permission of Lerner Publishing Group, Inc., except for the inclusion of brief quotations in an acknowledged review.

Lerner Publications Company
A division of Lerner Publishing Group, Inc.
241 First Avenue North
Minneapolis, MN 55401 U.S.A.

Website address: www.lernerbooks.com

Library of Congress Cataloging-in-Publication Data

Brill, Marlene Targ.
    Barack Obama : president for a new era / by Marlene Targ Brill. — Rev. ed.
      p.   cm. — (Gateway biographies)
    Rev. ed. of: Barack Obama: working to make a difference / by Marlene Targ Brill. ©2006.
    Includes bibliographical references and index.
    ISBN-13: 978-1-57505-950-1 (lib. bdg. : alk. paper)
    1. Obama, Barack—Juvenile literature. 2. African American legislators—Biography—Juvenile literature. 3. Legislators—United States—Biography—Juvenile literature. 4. United States. Congress. Senate—Biography—Juvenile literature. 5. Racially mixed people—United States—Biography—Juvenile literature. I. Title. II. Series: Gateway biography.
E901.1.O23B75 2009
328.73'092—dc22   2005016298

Manufactured in the United States of America
4 5 6 7 8 9 – BP – 14 13 12 11 10 09

CONTENTS

Obama and his family *(left to right)*—daughters, Natasha (called Sasha) and Malia, and wife, Michelle—greet the crowd in Chicago on election night.

On November 4, 2008, more than two hundred thousand people packed Chicago's Grant Park. Blacks, whites, young, old, and all races and religions came together. Many had captured their patch of grass early that morning. They wanted to be part of history.

Standing shoulder to shoulder, anxious audience members stayed glued to the giant television monitors broadcasting the voting results of the presidential election. The crowd's mood was electric. One by one, the states reported. As a state was announced for Senator Barack Obama, well-wishers erupted in cheers.

When all the polls closed, reporters called the election for Barack Obama. A lightning bolt of excitement shot through the crowd. People hugged, waved U.S. flags, and chanted "Yes We Can," Obama's campaign slogan. Many, especially blacks, cried tears of joy. At one time, in many places in the United States, African Americans were blocked from voting. This day, for the first time, a black man became president of the United States. Every child of color saw that they, too, could become president if they worked hard. "It is a new day in America," said Rep. John Lewis of Georgia, the famed civil rights activist.

The crowd roared as the new first family—Barack Obama; his wife, Michelle; and their daughters, ten-year-old Malia and seven-year-old Natasha, known as Sasha—walked onstage. Obama flashed a smile that spread ear to ear.

He turned serious as he spoke to voters. He repeated his campaign messages of hope, change, and unity. "This is our time, . . . to reclaim the American dream and reaffirm that fundamental truth, that out of many, we are one; that while we breathe, we hope. And where we are met with cynicism and doubts and those who tell us that we can't, we will respond with that timeless creed that sums up the spirit of a people: Yes we can."

The joy at Obama's election could be felt around the country. People poured into streets to celebrate together. Before this night, many of the same people doubted he had a chance to win. Besides his rousing speech at the 2004 Democratic convention, the Illinois senator seemed an unlikely candidate. The African American senator was not widely known. He had grown up with his single mother in two very different cultures and with little money. He had never run for such a high office.

But he spread his message of hope anyway. He called for change in politics as usual. Where did he get these ideas? How did this relative unknown capture the dreams of a nation? What led him to become the forty-fourth president of the United States?

The seeds of Obama's beliefs were planted during his multiethnic upbringing. "It was a wonderful childhood in the sense that I saw the world very early," he told a *Chicago Sun-Times* reporter.

Barack was born on August 4, 1961, in Honolulu, Hawaii. His mother, Stanley Ann Dunham, was a white woman from the Midwest. His father, Barack Obama, was a black man from Africa. They named their baby Barack, meaning "blessing from God."

"My name comes from Kenya, and my accent comes from Kansas," the younger Obama liked to explain.

Grassy plains stretch across most of Kansas. Obama's mother, Stanley Ann, grew up in this heartland state.

Barack's roots spread far and wide. On his mother's side alone, family history blended antislavery Kansans and Cherokee Indians with Scottish and Irish blood. Stanley Ann's birthplace in Wichita, Kansas, lay in the heart of the United States. People from Kansas in the 1940s were generally plainspoken and hardworking.

When Stanley Ann was born, her father, also Stanley, wanted a son. But the child turned out to be a girl. Always stubborn, Stanley gave the baby his name anyway and added the Ann. Stanley Ann grew up after World War II (1939–1945), when the country took great pride in its tough soldiers. Her father, Stanley, served in the war, while her mother took a job in an aircraft factory. But strict rules set up different treatment of girls and boys. A manly name for a female triggered terrible teasing. Playmates called the little girl Stanley Steamer and Stan the Man. Stanley Ann soon dropped her first name and kept the Ann.

Cornfields and oil rigs provided Ann's father with his first jobs in Kansas. But he kept searching for better work. Ann's mother, Madelyn Dunham, supplied the common sense in the family. But she couldn't keep her restless husband in one place for long. The family moved often. They lived in Texas and then Seattle, Washington. Stanley sold furniture or found other odd jobs.

After Ann finished high school in Seattle, the family left for Hawaii. The Hawaiian Islands were about to become the fiftieth state. Honolulu, the capital, bustled with new hotels and stores. The first jet had taken off

An aerial photograph of downtown Honolulu taken in the 1960s shows the giant Diamond Head crater rising in the distance. Waves crash on the sandy shore.

from the island, returning with sun-loving tourists. The possibility of unlimited opportunity lured Stanley to the growing city. He found a job selling furniture.

The steady sunshine, spotless beaches, and views of the towering Diamond Head crater suited the Dunhams. They moved to a street with huge Chinese banyan and monkeypod trees. Once settled in their home, Stanley and Madelyn set out to find other freethinkers like themselves.

Honolulu offered a mix of people from nations throughout the Pacific Ocean. The Dunhams met Hawaiians from the islands. They also met neighbors with roots in Japan, the Philippines, and China, and whites like themselves from the U.S. mainland. Honolulu encouraged the mix of people. The city name means "a joining together," *hono*, and "shelter from the wind," *lulu*.

Ann enrolled in the University of Hawaii. During her first year, she studied Russian. In class the shy eighteen-year-old girl noticed a tall, dark student from Kenya named Barack Obama.

Obama of Kenya was born into the Luo tribe. The Luo were known for their smart people who often entered politics. His father, Hussein Onyango Obama, was a tribal elder. But the British ran Kenya as a colony at the time. Hussein worked as a cook for British officers throughout most of his son's childhood.

His son Barack Obama spent his early life in a poor village along Lake Victoria. He herded his father's goats. Wild antelope, hippos, and lions wandered on nearby plains. Once old enough, Obama attended an English-speaking school in a tin-roof shack. The colonial government had set up these schools around the country. From the beginning, his sharp mind stood out in class. With time, he earned a scholarship to a better school in Nairobi.

While Obama studied in Nairobi, Kenya gained independence from Great Britain. Kenyan leaders established a joint education program with the United States. The

Barack Obama, who was later to give his name to his son, grew up in a Kenyan village similar to this one on the shore of Lake Victoria.

Kenyan government sent the nation's most promising students to U.S. universities. In turn, the students agreed to return to Africa with the latest information. That way, Kenya could benefit from the students' education.

Twenty-three-year-old Obama was chosen to attend the University of Hawaii. In 1959 he became the school's first African student. He studied economics and earned top grades. But most classmates knew him for speaking out

Ann Dunham met Barack Obama of Kenya in class at the University of Hawaii *(above)*.

in support of other foreign students. Together, they created the university's International Students Association. Members voted Obama as their president.

While in Russian class, Obama was drawn to the generous, easygoing, and intelligent Ann. They debated politics and the economy. They talked about terrible clashes over race in the United States. Southern whites expected blacks to sit in the back of buses and use separate bathrooms, water fountains, and schools. Many towns prevented blacks from voting and dating whites. Obama never understood the inequality in such a great nation. Even Kenyans had earned the right to walk with whom they wanted and go where they pleased.

Ann invited Barack Obama home to meet her parents. Madelyn and Stanley took to his charm and quick mind. Ann and Barack grew closer and soon fell in love. They married in 1960, a bold move. At that time, half the states in the country banned mixed marriages. If the couple had traveled together, he could have been attacked or even hanged. But Ann's parents supported the young couple. Barack and Ann and her parents adopted the color-blind attitude that Hawaii represented.

The newlyweds lived with Stanley and Madelyn while they finished school. Within a year, little Barack, nick-named Barry, was born. As grandparents, Stanley and Madelyn preferred the names Gramps and Toot, short for *tutu*, the Hawaiian word for "grandmother." From the beginning, they doted on their grandson. But a baby strained family finances. Madelyn found a job as secretary for a bank to help pay the extra bills.

Two years later, Barry's father graduated. He completed a four-year program in three years and came out at the top of his class. Harvard University gave him a scholarship to continue his education. But there was one hitch. The school offered just enough money to cover one student. Ann and the baby had to stay behind.

After Harvard, Barry's father returned to Kenya. He had a duty to the country that had sent him overseas. He also had responsibility for his Kenyan wife and children. In Luo custom, a man could marry more than one woman as long as he cared for them and their children. Ann disliked this custom. Barry's parents divorced.

For years, Barry knew his father through old photos and family stories only. His grandparents fed him tales of his father's brilliance. They talked about his father's commitment to bettering the world. His mother reassured Barry that his brains came from his father. Even with these stories, many questions about his father nagged at Barry. Ann, Gramps, and Toot showered Barry with love. Still, he felt something was missing in his life.

A TALE OF TWO HOMELANDS

Barry grew up much as a Hawaiian American boy. He ate sashimi (sliced raw fish), a taro root paste called poi, and rice candy made with wrappers that could be eaten.

Barry grew up on the Hawaiian island of Oahu, which is ringed with sandy beaches.

He learned to swim and bodysurf in the shimmering blue green and purple waters off Sandy Beach. His grandfather took him to watch astronauts land at Hickam Air Force Base. They spearfished at Kailua Bay.

When Barry turned six, his world totally changed. His mother married another foreign student from the university. This new husband was an Indonesian named Lolo Soetoro. Lolo had visited their house for the past two years, and everyone liked him. He was shorter than Barry's father and had thick dark hair and an easy smile. Barry found Lolo to be a calm man who made time to wrestle with him and play chess with Gramps. But Barry had no idea what to expect when his mother announced they were going to Jakarta, the capital of Indonesia, to live with Lolo.

After arriving in Indonesia, Lolo drove them past villages that faded into forest and boys riding water buffalo in a brown river. Tiny stores and one-storied whitewashed homes lined the dirt road leading toward Lolo's house. The family's first home was at the edge of town. Barry went from a house in busy Hawaii to a small, red stucco-and-tile house that bordered a jungle. Squawking chickens and ducks, a large beige dog, two birds of paradise, a white cockatoo, two baby crocodiles, and a pet gibbon named Tata roamed the backyard.

Moving to Indonesia seemed like a great adventure to Barry. His first night in the new home,

OBAMA SAYS HIS FAVORITE BOOK as a child was *Where the Wild Things Are* by Maurice Sendak.

Barry included stories from his childhood in his autobiography, *Dreams from My Father.*

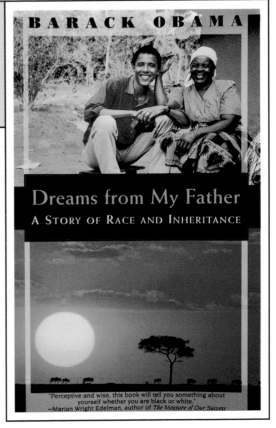

Barry watched Lolo's servant lop off the head of a chicken for their welcome dinner. At bedtime Barry slept under a mosquito net in the open house. He fell asleep to the sound of chirping crickets. "I could hardly believe my good fortune," he remembered in his autobiography, *Dreams from My Father.*

Lolo worked as a geologist, and Ann taught English at the U.S. Embassy. When together, Lolo treated Barry as his own son. He bought Barry boxing gloves so he could learn to defend himself. He introduced Barry to local dishes of "dog meat (tough), snake meat (tougher), and roasted grasshopper (crunchy)." Lolo taught Barry about his beliefs in Islam and animal powers and how to deal with endless streams of street beggars.

Indonesia proved a much different place from the beautiful land of aloha. Jakarta's downtown streets were a jumble of *becaks* (transport bicycles) motorcycles, carts, and a few cars. Barry saw waist-deep floods during rainy seasons. Other times, the beating sun turned rice and cassava fields to dust. Barry played with kites, watched cockfights, and tramped barefoot through muddy farms. At home he took cold baths, battled mosquitoes, and used a hole in the ground for a toilet. Poverty, disease, and signs of deep divisions between rich and poor showed everywhere.

Lolo and Ann couldn't afford private school with other Americans for Barry. He attended local school with children of servants and farmers. It was a Catholic school in a Muslim country. The school gave Barry different understandings of religion and life. Within six months, Barry mastered Indonesia's language and customs.

Ann worried about Barry's education. She sent for teaching supplies from the United States to build on his schoolwork. Ann woke Barry at four in the morning every school day. She practiced lessons with her sleepy son for three hours before his class. Ann peppered each lesson with her sense of positive midwestern values. She told her son to always be honest and fair, show good judgment, and have faith in himself to chart his own future.

"If you want to grow into a human being, you're going to need some values," she told him.

After four years, the added lessons were not enough for Ann. She feared Indonesia could become a dangerous place. Moreover, she and Lolo were experiencing problems with their marriage. Ann decided Barry

Barry often explored Jakarta's busy streets with his mother and her new husband, Lolo.

should attend private school in Honolulu and live with Gramps and Toot. She and Maya, his baby sister, would soon follow.

SCHOOL YEARS

At the age of ten, Barry returned to Honolulu. Getting off the plane, Barry noticed more gray hairs on Gramps and Toot. Other changes had occurred while he and his mother were gone. Gramps now sold life insurance, although without much success. Toot had risen to bank vice president, the first woman to do so. The two led a quieter social life than they had four years earlier. They lived in a two-bedroom apartment in a high-rise building overlooking University Avenue and Diamond Head crater.

Their apartment was in walking distance of Punahou School, Barry's new school. Classes from kindergarten through twelfth grade were held at the school's seventy-six-acre campus. Students from various ethnic and religious populations attended, although most were white. Barry's grandparents were proud that their grandchild had received a scholarship. Punahou School was one of the largest and most respected private schools in the nation.

Barry entered fifth grade in fall of 1971. He wore sandals from Indonesia and outdated clothes chosen by Gramps. Barry was one of the few new students and only one of two blacks in his grade. He felt totally out of place. After a few rocky months, he adjusted and gained friends. Barry never let on that questions about race and his parents gnawed at him.

"He was a good student. A nice, happy-go-lucky kid who knew how to stand up for himself," remembered Pal Eldredge, Barry's math and science teacher.

Barry spent seven years at Punahou. In the early days, the chubby student stood out as a friendly boy who spoke up in class. He seemed curious, always asking questions. Barry maintained a B-plus grade average, and he participated in many activities, some mischievous.

Barry *(back row, third from left)* moved back to Hawaii to attend fifth grade at Punahou School.

"Barry wrote his name in wet cement on campus by the cafeteria," said Eric Kusunoki, his homeroom teacher throughout high school. "Everyone knows who he is."

Basketball fever grabbed Barry during his high school years. His father, Barack, had sent him a basketball as a present. He bounced it on the way to school and in hallways going from class to class. He practiced all the time. When others stayed in the cafeteria during ninety-degree days, Barry shot hoops on the school's steamy black asphalt court.

Barry, wearing number 23, goes up for a shot. Barry's love of playing basketball finally earned him a spot on his high school basketball team.

"He was what we call a gym rat," explained coach Chris McLachlin. "He loved the game so much that he'd do anything to practice. He snuck past teachers when they opened the gym's locked doors. When no one was around, he broke into the gym."

Barry made the basketball team his last two years at Punahou. By then he came closer to his six-foot-two adult height. The team won second place in the state his first year on the team and first place during his senior year. Barry played forward on an exceptional team, which meant he competed for floor time during games. As Barry was the team's only left-hander, Coach McLachlin sent him out for sure whenever other left-handers played. Barry wore a number 23 jersey before Michael Jordan, the famous basketball star, made the number popular. Both players lived for the game.

"Barry was competitive but very intellectual as well. He understood the game and complicated plays," said Coach McLachlin. "Had it not been that cycle (of players), he would have been a star. I really admired the fact that he loved the game so much."

AS A CHILD, Barack wanted to be an astronaut, then an architect, and then a basketball player.

In high school, Barry lived with Ann and his sister Maya. They rented a small apartment one block from school on Beretania Street. Ann returned to the university to obtain a master's degree in anthropology, the study of people from different places and cultures. She received grants to help pay her way, but money and time remained tight. Barry helped out whenever he could. He watched his sister, grocery shopped, washed clothes, and took a job scooping ice cream. When Ann needed to return to Indonesia for her fieldwork, Barry chose to live with his grandparents again. He thought he'd been uprooted enough.

Despite basketball and a good family and school, Barry appeared headed for trouble. Confusion over race stalked him. He and the few blacks who attended Punahou shared their anger over racial slights they experienced. A bad joke about color rubbing off that wasn't funny. Name-calling. A white woman's fearful look when they shared an elevator.

Bottled-up feelings and high school experimenting led Barry to try drugs. He stopped short of anything

Barry's senior yearbook picture from Punahou School, the well-respected private school in Honolulu that he had attended since fifth grade

lasting and serious, and his schoolwork never suffered. But those days preyed on him later. "Junkie, pot-head. That's where I'd been headed: the final, fatal role of the young would-be black man," Obama wrote.

To better understand what was happening to him, Barry read books. He studied famous authors to learn how they dealt with being black in a white-powered country. He worked to find his place in a family that was both black and white. He tried to accept himself. He tried not to feel so alone.

FINDING DIRECTION

Barry wasn't particularly interested in college. He chose Occidental College in Los Angeles because he had met a girl from there during the summer. The school of under two thousand students turned into a good choice. The hillside campus was beautiful with its palm trees, white buildings, and red-tiled roofs. And Occidental gave Barry his first taste of politics.

Students around the country protested the mistreatment of blacks in South Africa. They wanted their colleges to stop conducting business with the racist white government there. Barry gave a speech to drum up interest in the cause at Occidental. For the first time, he felt the power of his words to change minds. He connected with the international black movement. As he claimed his voice and black identity, he reclaimed his Kenyan name, Barack.

OBAMA HAS ALWAYS BEEN A BIG READER. He formed many of his ideas and goals after reading authors such as James Baldwin, Toni Morrison, and Ernest Hemingway.

After two years at Occidental, Barack became restless. He wrote to his father about visiting Kenya after graduation. Needing a change, he took advantage of an exchange program between Occidental and Columbia University. In the fall of 1981, Barack moved to New York City and enrolled at Columbia. A different environment of honking horns, crowded streets and subways, and twenty-four-hour activity greeted him. Barack had never seen such a city. New Yorkers moved to their own beats—fast and faster.

Barack thrived on the change of pace. "I ran three miles a day and fasted on Sundays. For the first time, I

applied myself to my studies and started keeping a journal of daily reflections and bad poetry," he wrote.

Two years later, Barack Obama graduated with a
degree in political science, the study of how politics and
government work. By then he had received word that his
father died in a car accident in Kenya. Obama put aside
thoughts of visiting Africa—at least for the time being.

POUNDING THE PAVEMENT

After college Obama looked for a job as a community
organizer. He wanted to promote civil rights at the
grassroots, neighborhood level. When no organizing
job developed, he took a position as research assistant
for a large company. He had college loans to repay. He
needed savings because organizers earned low salaries.

While Obama was at the company, Auma, his Kenyan
half sister, called. She asked to visit him in New York.
He knew Auma, who studied in Germany, only through
a few letters. Meeting blood relatives excited him. Just
before Auma's arrival, however, she called again. Their
younger brother, David, had died in a motorcycle accident. She must return to Kenya instead. Barack tried
to ease her sorrow. But he felt confused about his own
feelings for a stepbrother he had never met.

In 1985 an organizing job opened in Chicago.
Obama went to work for Developing Communities
Project, a small group in the city's far South Side. The

neighborhood had undergone a wave of plant closings and worker layoffs. Residents lacked jobs and lived in run-down apartments. Obama hoped to organize them to push for improving their living conditions.

Obama started his job filled with enthusiasm. But community organizing sometimes became a thankless job. In the beginning, Obama called meetings where few people showed. People living in housing projects focused on their next meal. They didn't have time or energy to tackle broader social issues. Obama refused to give up. He turned to churches to support his and the community's causes.

Residents walk past the LeClaire Courts housing project in Chicago. Obama hoped to help people in poorer communities improve their lives.

"He went from church to church, beating the pavement, trying to get every pastor in the community," the Reverend Alvin Love of Lilydale First Baptist Church told *StreetWise*. "This skinny, scrawny guy trying to find out how we can make the community better. He just walked the streets."

After several disappointments, Obama experienced small successes. He helped bring job-training programs to poor neighborhoods. He gathered a busload of parents from a housing project and drove them to the downtown Chicago Housing Authority office. With Obama's support, they insisted on the removal of asbestos from their apartments. Used in many old buildings, this material had been discovered to be dangerous.

With time, the people he helped and Chicago's close-knit neighborhoods and lakefront parks and museums grew on Obama. He often felt discouraged by the snail's pace of change. But this only fueled his desire to do more for the everyday

> **OBAMA'S HEROES ARE Martin Luther King Jr., Mahatma Gandhi, and Cesar Chavez. They all believed in bringing about change through peaceful means.**

folks he met. Obama realized that he had choices the others did not have. Maybe they came from his family's support. Maybe they came from his being exposed to a larger world than a single run-down neighborhood. Maybe his choices stemmed from how smart and thoughtful he was. Whatever the reason, the more Obama met people in need, the more his desire to help them deepened.

Three years after arriving in Chicago, Obama applied to law schools. He hoped to gain tools that would help him bring about change. Several colleges accepted him. He chose Harvard University, his father's school.

FAMILY IN KENYA

Before leaving for school near Boston, Obama traveled to Kenya. He wanted to fill in the blanks about the father who had visited him only once, when Barack was ten years old. All Barack remembered of the man was how he dropped into their lives, barked orders, and left forever. Before he left, Barack's father said he expected big things of his son. To the little boy, his father seemed an imposing man with bony knees and a deep, sure voice. Yet his hearty laugh and love of music filled a room. Obama wanted to understand more about this mystery man. He wanted to learn about the land of his roots.

In Kenya, Obama toured the capital of Nairobi. Peddlers in the old marketplace hawked wooden trinkets and jewelry. Women wrapped in bright cloth with shaven heads and beaded earrings carried goods

BARACK WAS RAISED WITH KNOWLEDGE OF many religions. As an adult, he found great comfort in religion, and he says he has deep faith. He became a Christian at Trinity United Church of Christ in Chicago.

On his trip to Kenya, Obama met his step-grandmother, Sarah Onyango Obama, and two stepbrothers. Obama pieced together part of his past by connecting with family members.

on their heads. He visited aunts, uncles, and cousins on the outskirts of the city. He met his Kenyan step-grandmother in Kisumu, a sleepy town on the savanna along Lake Victoria. Auma introduced Barack to his stepbrothers Roy and Bernard.

Over the next month, Barack Obama pieced together his African history. He learned about his father's high-level government job as an economist. He heard about his fall from grace after he bucked corrupt officials. With each story, Barack understood more about his father's princely pride and great generosity. Then he cried at his father's grave. He made peace with the man and larger-than-life stories from his childhood. Barack Obama left Kenya with a stronger feeling of himself and where he belonged in the world.

BREAKING BARRIERS

Obama entered Harvard University in the fall of 1988. "On first impression, he seemed older than he was," recalled Kenneth Mack, former classmate and current Harvard professor of law. "I thought of him as a black guy with a Midwestern accent. But he seemed experienced in the world in ways some of us weren't. He spoke well and concisely in a way that seemed wise and broad-minded."

The first year of law school required lots of studying. To unwind, Obama shot baskets as he had always done. Basketball star Michael Jordan, number 23, became his symbol of focus, hard work, and competition.

At the end of his first year, Obama made *Harvard Law Review*. He would write and edit articles for this journal for legal scholars. Serving on the *Review* was one of the highest honors for law students. After a year on the job, all the editors chose Obama as president of the *Review*. He became the first African American to receive such recognition.

In 1989 Obama was selected for the *Harvard Law Review*. A year later, he was elected its president.

The announcement produced a flurry of media attention. A publishing company contracted with Obama to write the story of his life. Doors opened to leading law firms.

The summer before graduation, Barack clerked at a large Chicago law firm. He discovered that he disliked

Michelle Robinson's Harvard yearbook photo. Barack and Michelle met in Chicago and fell in love.

the cutthroat atmosphere of high-powered corporate law for wealthy clients. But he did like Chicago. He felt at home there. After Harvard, Obama returned to Chicago to look for work.

Part of the reason for Obama's return involved a new woman in his life. Michelle Robinson was the lawyer responsible for showing him around the firm that summer. Robinson was a tall, attractive Princeton graduate who received her law degree from Harvard before Obama did. Michelle proved to be thoughtful, bright, and totally frank, a perfect match for Barack. The two married in 1992.

The couple moved into the mixed-race Hyde Park neighborhood on Chicago's South Side. Obama joined a small firm that focused on civil rights. He worked on legal cases about job discrimination and low-income housing. He and his clients worked to improve public health and the environment.

In 1992 Obama added the Illinois Project Vote to his workload. Under his direction, the project encouraged 150,000 new voters from poor neighborhoods to register to vote. This would give them a voice in elections. Evenings, Obama taught classes in constitutional law at the University of Chicago.

"He stood out in everything he did. He worked in court. He wrote briefs," said his law firm boss Judson Miner. "Barack is an extraordinarily talented person with an extraordinary set of values in every respect. It was clear early on that he was going to be pressured at some point to jump into government or politics."

RUNNING FOR PUBLIC OFFICE

Obama made no secret of wanting to run for public office. He mentioned the subject to friends at Harvard. He talked about it while at the law firm. In 1996 State Senator Alice Palmer handed Obama his chance to become an elected politician. She decided to run for Congress and drafted him to fill her slot as state senator. Palmer's Thirteenth Congressional District included wealthier blacks and whites from the University of Chicago area, where Barack and Michelle lived. It also extended into the poor, mainly black regions farther south, where Obama had worked during his organizing days.

As Obama's campaign fired up, Palmer changed her mind. She had lost the primary election to represent her party and wanted her job back. Obama refused, saying she promised not to run. Besides, his campaign was already hot. Obama's workers challenged Palmer's petitions to run. The resulting battle caused Palmer to withdraw from the race. The setback ended her career in politics.

Obama wound up winning the race for state senator. But the situation caused hard feelings. Many felt he should have stepped aside. Palmer was older and didn't have many more chances to serve, whereas he did.

Four years later, Obama faced a similar situation. He believed that the sitting U.S. representative, Bobby Rush, wasn't doing enough for his district. He jumped into the race to unseat the four-time winner. This time, Obama lost. Rush whipped him two to one in the primary. Obama finally learned his lesson. He vowed to take politics slower. He had a lot to learn about state government before he tackled national politics. The Illinois senator focused on improving conditions for his South Side supporters. Still, the two races hinted at how driven—and impatient—he really was.

For seven years, Obama fought on behalf of working families in the Illinois Senate. He chaired the public health and welfare committee. In this position, he introduced more than 780 bills. About 280 became law. Under Obama's leadership, state government expanded insurance programs for twenty thousand additional children and sixty-five thousand more families in Illinois. He helped reduce taxes for working families. He ushered in a bill to further protect women from abuse. His

Obama speaks at a debate on legislation about immigrant driver's licenses at the state capitol in Springfield, Illinois, on November 6, 2003. He served in the Illinois Senate for seven years before being elected to a national office.

boldest move, however, involved another law-enforcement bill. He led the call for ground-breaking rules that required police to videotape the questioning of murder suspects.

To accomplish so much, Obama needed the respect of other state representatives. He had a gift for reaching out to opponents to find agreement. "What drove him were policy issues," said Miner. "But he realized that government involves compromise. Barack was so talented that he compromised from a position of strength."

NATIONAL OFFICE

In April 2003, U.S. Senator Peter Fitzgerald of Illinois decided against running for a second term. Barack saw his

OBAMA ENCOURAGES CHILDREN TO BE INTERESTED and involved in politics. He told *Scholastic News* reporters that "politics really ends up having an impact on your lives whether you like it or not. If you look at who (decides) how much money will be going to (your school), that's a political decision."

chance to run for national office. This time, Obama quickly shot ahead of others in his party. He easily beat six opponents in the primary, winning 53 percent of the vote.

"We confounded a lot of odds that said that whites won't vote for blacks, or those in suburbs won't vote for a city guy or downstate people won't vote for folks from upstate," Obama told a PBS reporter.

After the primary, the Republican front-runner, Jack Ryan, withdrew from the race over a family scandal. State Republicans brought a black former ambassador named Alan Keyes from out of state. Keyes tore through the state like a bulldog. He attacked Obama on all levels—his ideas, his character, anything he said.

Obama stuck to running a positive race. He spoke of hope and unity. His motto was "Yes we can." Compared to Keyes, Obama seemed better than reasonable. He already proved he could get jobs done in state government. He connected with all kinds of people in and out of government.

The turning point came with Obama's stirring speech at the 2004 Democratic National Convention. Thirty-five thousand people saw him deliver a powerful speech.

Millions more listened on television and radio.

In this speech, Obama introduced himself as "the skinny guy with big ears and a funny name." He told of his family, their roots in different cultures, and their hardships. More important, he explained their common dreams for their children and their high hopes for a better life in the United States. "I stand here knowing that my story is part of the larger American story," he said.

Obama talked about U.S. problems too. Some government leaders hoped to split the country by wealth, race, or religion. He called for Americans to come together. "I say tonight . . . there's not a black America and white America and Latino America and Asian America. There's

Thousands of supporters held up Barack Obama signs to cheer on the U.S. Senate candidate from Illinois during his keynote address at the Democratic National Convention in July 2004.

the United States of America. In the end, that is . . . (the) greatest gift to us, . . . a belief in things not seen, a belief that there are better days ahead."

After his moving speech, Obama's star power soared. Keyes didn't have a chance after that. Obama won a sweeping victory with 70 percent of the vote. He became only the fifth black U.S. senator in history. Invitations poured in for him to speak to various groups. He received many awards, including the NAACP (National Association for the Advancement of Colored People) Fight for Freedom Award. Obama's publisher offered him a three-book deal worth $1.9 million.

"It took a lot of blood, sweat, and tears to get to where we are today, but we have just begun," Obama wrote in a blog. Supporters agreed. Many expressed great hopes for his future. Some called him the Great Black Hope or a rising star. Internet sites offered "Obama for '08 President" bumper stickers and posters. People in the Kenyan province where his father came from expressed similar high hopes. African parents named babies and an elementary school after Barack.

As junior Illinois senator and a newcomer, however, Obama ranked ninety-ninth out of one hundred in the Senate pecking order. His ability to effect change would be limited, at least at the beginning. First, he had to set up his tiny basement office and "learn to find his way around the building."

FOR GOOD LUCK on election days, Obama starts the day by playing basketball.

As Obama settled into his new job, a few things became clear to him. He noticed how little government served ordinary, struggling people. And he saw how divided the government and the nation had become. After two years in Congress, the restless senator decided government needed to change to better serve its citizens. The citizens, he believed, needed hope.

Meanwhile, interest in Obama never slowed. The pressure on him to produce change became overwhelming. In 2007 he announced that he would campaign to become the Democratic nominee for president. Many people worried that the stress of a run for president would spoil him. He would get so caught up in winning that he would forget why he originally entered politics.

Many more, like Judson Miner, disagreed. "He has good judgment. He will not let things that matter the least get in the way of those that matter most," Miner said. "Barack wants to make a difference."

Obama announced his candidacy for president in Springfield, Illinois, in February 2007.

MR. PRESIDENT

Obama ran against a strong group of Democrats, including U.S. Senator Hillary Clinton of New York, the first woman to become a major contender for the presidency. After a long and challenging campaign, Obama became the Democratic nominee for president in 2008. His nomination was a historic event. No other African American had ever reached so high in politics. His Republican challenger was longtime senator John McCain of Arizona.

Obama ran an organized campaign that focused on the average citizen. The United States was involved in two wars—in Iraq and Afghanistan—and the economy was tanking. People were losing homes, banks were failing, and gas prices were rising. Obama listened to their pain and offered ways to make life better. Moreover, he ran a positive campaign.

Democratic hopefuls Hillary Clinton and Obama took part in a debate during the primaries in April 2008.

Obama and Republican presidential nominee John McCain *(middle)* debate in October 2008. CBS television journalist Bob Schieffer *(right)* moderated the debate.

Voters connected with Obama's message of hope and change. He was the first candidate to make effective use of the Internet for a campaign. He talked directly to potential voters through e-mails, blogs, and text messages, and they responded by volunteering and donating more than $600 million, a new record.

On November 4, 2008, Election Day, 53 percent of voters chose Obama compared with 46 percent for John McCain. Obama became the forty-fourth president of the United States. He was the first African American and first Hawaiian-born president. His election signaled a sea of change in politics. Blacks, Hispanics, and new voters felt for the first time that their vote counted, and they turned out in larger numbers than in any other election.

Barack Obama is sworn in as the 44th president of the United States on January 20, 2009.

Throughout the campaign, even-tempered Obama talked about being imperfect—an imperfect father, husband, and public servant. On election night, he warned that as president, he might not please everyone. But in his moving message of hope, he urged everyone to always keep trying, to always keep working toward higher goals. Above all, he hoped the people would join him in working to make a difference in the lives of others. A new era began in the United States.

IMPORTANT DATES

1961   Born on August 4 in Honolulu, Hawaii

1967   Moves with his mother and new stepfather to Jakarta, Indonesia

1971   Returns to Hawaii and enrolls at Punahou School

1979   Graduates from Punahou School and enters Occidental College in Los Angeles

1981   Switches to Columbia University in New York City

1983   Graduates from Columbia University with a degree in political science

1985   Begins a three-year job as community organizer in Chicago

1988   Starts Harvard Law School in Cambridge, Massachusetts

1990   Elected the first black president of *Harvard Law Review*

1991	Graduates from Harvard Law School magna cum laude, with high honors
1992	Joins a Chicago law firm to work on civil rights cases Marries Michelle Robinson
1995	Publishes *Dreams from My Father*
1996	Wins election for Illinois state senator
1998	Rejoices in birth of daughter Malia Ann
2000	Loses to Bobby Rush in the primary for U.S. representative from Illinois by a two-to-one margin
2001	Cheers birth of second daughter, Natasha, known as Sasha
2004	Elected U.S. senator from Illinois, becoming the fifth African American in history to join the Senate
2005	Receives the NAACP Fight for Freedom Award as well as its Chairman's Award
2006	Publishes *The Audacity of Hope: Thoughts on Reclaiming the American Dream*

2007	Announces that he will seek the Democratic nomination for president
2008	Chosen to run for president as the Democratic Party nominee
2009	Becomes the first African American president of the United States.

FURTHER READING

Davis, William. *Barack Obama: The Politics of Hope.* Stockton, NJ: OTTN Publishers, 2007.

Grimes, Nikki, and Bryan Collier. *Barack Obama: Son of Promise, Child of Hope.* New York: Simon & Schuster, 2008.

Official Obama Website
http://www.BarackObama.com

Sapet, Kerrily. *Barack Obama.* Greensboro, NC: Morgan Reynolds Publishing, 2007.

Wagner, Heather Lehr. *Barack Obama.* New York: Checkmark Books, 2008.

The White House
http://www.whitehouse.gov

INDEX